THE MOUNTAIN STILL SPEAKS

VOLUME III

STILL HE SPEAKS

ECHOES FROM THE HIGHER GROUND,
THE NARROW WAY, THE SECRET
LIFE, AND THE ROCK THAT STANDS

DAMIANO B. CENTOLA

EXPLORA BOOKS
700 – 838 West Hastings St. Vancouver
BC V6C 0A6
www.explorabooks.com
Phone: (604) 330 6795

No part of this book may be reproduced, stored in a retrieval system, or transmitted by any means without the written permission of the author.

Because of the dynamic nature of the Internet, any web addresses or links contained in this book may have changed since publication and may no longer be valid. The views expressed in this work are solely those of the author and do not necessarily reflect the views of the publisher, and the publisher hereby disclaims any responsibility for them.

Bible verses are quoted from the King James Version (KJV), which is public domain, the English Standard Version (ESV), and the New King James Version (NKJV).

ISBN: 978-1-83430-044-3 *(Paperback)*
978-1-83430-045-0 *(Hardback)*
978-1-83430-046-7 *(eBook)*

© 2025 Damiano B. Centola. All rights reserved.

THE MOUNTAIN STILL SPEAKS

VOLUME III

Table of Contents

Preface i

Chapter I 1

Chapter II 7

Chapter III 15

Chapter IV 23

Chapter V 31

Chapter VI 39

Chapter VII 47

Chapter VIII 55

Chapter IX 63

Chapter X 71

Chapter XI 79

Chapter XII 87

Chapter XIII 95

Chapter XIV 103

About the Author 119

Preface

The Secret Life, the Narrow Way, and the Rock That Stands The Sermon continues. Not because Jesus spoke longer than three chapters, but because His words never stopped echoing. The wind that brushed the Galilean mountain still stirs the hearts of those who listen. And those who dare follow Him higher find that the slope narrows, the crowd thins, and the Word cuts even deeper.

This is not where the Sermon begins.
This is where it pierces.
Beyond the beatitudes, past the outer laws, deeper than religious routines—Christ now speaks to the secret life. To the voice behind the voice. To the vow made in the dark. To the silence that either trembles before God or hides from Him.

The Mountain Still Speaks, Volume III explores this sacred terrain.
Not the public life, but the hidden one.
Not the wide road, but the narrow path.
Not the sand, but the Rock.

This is for the disciple who's ready to lose everything false and find the one thing true. For the one who's weary of spiritual performance and hungry for presence. For those who want not just to act holy, but to become holy—in private, in silence, in truth.

As you ascend these pages, may you be stripped, refined, and filled.

Not with noise, but with fire.

Not with effort, but with presence.

Not with applause, but with the approval of Heaven.

Still He speaks.

Still He calls.

Still He waits for you—on higher ground.

— Damiano B. Centola

Chapter I
Let Your Yes Be Yes
— Truth in Speech

"But let your communication be, Yea, yea; Nay, nay: for whatsoever is more than these cometh of evil."
— Matthew 5:37 (KJV)

The mountain had grown steeper.
Not in elevation, but in demand.

What began with blessings— "Blessed are the poor in spirit, the meek, the peacemakers…"—now ascended into the depths of character, into the marrow of discipleship, into the realm of hidden integrity. Jesus was not content to address external behavior. He was going after what lies underneath: motive, intention, and the unseen architecture of the soul. And so He speaks directly—not to the Pharisees, but to the would-be followers of the Kingdom—with these nine unassuming words:

"Let your yes be yes, and your no, no."

To the casual ear, it sounded like common sense.
To the crowd on the hillside, it may have seemed minor.
But to those with spiritual ears, it thundered.

Because it wasn't about vocabulary.

It was about truth.

I. The Power of One Word

In Heaven, one word is enough.

God said, "Let there be light," and there was light.

Jesus said, "Follow Me," and the fishermen dropped their nets.

One "yes" from the King causes galaxies to spin.

One "no" from His mouth silences storms.

In a world where language has been polluted, Jesus reclaims it.

He teaches that in the Kingdom, truth must be simple. Not simplistic—simple.

No religious performance. No manipulative additions.

No embellishment to make a statement sound stronger than it is.

> "Let your communication be, Yea, yea; Nay, nay…"
>
> "…for whatsoever is more than these cometh of evil."

That "more" is the place where deception grows.

That "more" is the home of showmanship, exaggeration, and self-justification.

He is not merely talking about speech.

He is confronting the human desire to appear truthful without being truthful.

II. Swearing to Cover Up Weak Character

In first-century Judaism, it became customary to "swear by" things to prove sincerity.

Some would swear by the gold of the temple.

Others by the altar.

Others by Jerusalem.

The more sacred the object, the more believable the vow.

But the point was not reverence—it was manipulation.

People wanted to sound holy while reserving the right to break their word.

So, Jesus says, "Swear not at all."

Not because every vow is wicked, but because every false vow is.

The more we lean on dramatic language to make ourselves sound believable, the more we reveal the absence of integrity. If we were known to be truthful, we wouldn't need to dress our words with divine wrapping paper.

III. Integrity Is Measured in the Mundane

The Kingdom of Heaven doesn't wait for a courtroom to test your truth.

It watches what you say to your spouse in the kitchen.

It listens when you make promises to your children.

It pays attention when you say you'll call back.

It hears your "I'll pray for you" and waits to see if you ever do.

Truth is not only tested in public—it is proved in private.

The call to let your yes be yes and your no be no is not a lesson in diction.

It is a demand for wholeness.

A man whose "yes" can't be trusted needs oaths.

A woman whose "no" is flexible requires props.

But those who belong to the Light walk-in clarity.

They do not stutter when they mean to stand.

They do not layer their language with extra weight.

Their words carry weight because their life does.

IV. The Evil in the Extra

"Anything more than this comes from evil."

This is the part most overlook.

Jesus links exaggerated speech to evil. Why?

Because every lie—however small—has spiritual lineage.

The serpent in Eden did not bite Eve.

He twisted truth. He stretched it. He added to it.

He took God's pure words and made them sound slightly off.

That's what Jesus warns against.

Not only direct lying.

But the subtle inflation of speech that draws attention to self and away from God.

The added oath, the dramatic tone, the religious lingo—all of it becomes a theater of credibility.

And Heaven does not reward actors.

V. Let Speech Reflect the Nature of the King

Jesus is the Living Word.

And in Him, there is no shadow of turning.

When He speaks, it is not to impress.

It is to illuminate.

He says "yes" and creation responds.

He says "no" and demons flee.

So must it be with His disciples.

We are not called to swear by heaven, because Heaven is His throne.

We are not to swear by the earth, for it is His footstool.

Even the hairs on our head are numbered—we cannot control even that.

If we cannot govern the physical, we certainly have no right to invoke the divine to give weight to our wavering hearts.

Therefore:

Speak plainly.

Speak purely.

Speak as if God is listening—because He is.

VI. Why Simplicity Is Holiness

There is a dignity in directness.

There is a beauty in simplicity.

And there is a spiritual weight behind every word you speak.

When you say "yes," let the Spirit bear witness.

When you say "no," let the peace of God stand with it.

You do not need extra words to sound powerful.

The presence of God in your life is what gives your speech authority.

The early Church didn't swear.

They spoke, and signs followed.

Because their "yes" was holy.

Their "no" was sacred.

And their words carried the scent of Heaven.

VII. The Bride Must Speak Like Her Groom

We are the Bride of Christ.

And the Bride does not speak carelessly.

She does not make promises she will not keep.

She does not flatter, manipulate, or pretend.

Her words are pure.

Her commitments are firm.

Her voice is steady—because she reflects the One whose Word is eternal.

In the final hour, there will be many voices.

Some loud, some persuasive, some poetic.

But only one will sound like Truth.

And that is the voice of the Bride—who has been formed by fire, trained by silence, and shaped by the mountain.

VIII. Conclusion: Let the Mountain Form Your Mouth

So let your yes be yes.

Let your no be no.

Say what you mean, and mean what you say.

Let your mouth be an altar—not for performance, but for truth.

God is not looking for perfect speakers.

He is looking for pure ones.

Let the mountain shape your tongue.

Let Heaven govern your tone.

Let the Spirit sanctify your words.

And let every vow be unnecessary, because your life is already a testimony.

OATH

Damiano B. Centola

Chapter II
Do Not Swear at All
— The Vow and the Name

"But I say unto you, Swear not at all; neither by heaven; for it is God's throne: Nor by the earth; for it is his footstool: neither by Jerusalem; for it is the city of the great King. Neither shalt thou swear by thy head, because thou canst not make one hair white or black. But let your communication be, Yea, yea; Nay, nay: for whatsoever is more than these cometh of evil."

— Matthew 5:34–37 (KJV)

There are few places in the Sermon on the Mount where Jesus speaks with such abrupt finality.

"Swear not at all."

The command is absolute. It is not softened by cultural suggestion or grammatical nuance.

It is a divine interruption to a world addicted to oaths, embellishment, and performative speech. And in these verses, the Son of God reclaims the sacredness of His own Name, calling His people to speak with the clarity and purity of Heaven.

But to understand the force behind His words, we must descend into the religious theater of His time—a world where words were cheap and vows were tools for manipulation.

I. The Religious Game of Oaths

In first-century Jewish culture, vows were everywhere. The more elaborate the oath, the more serious the commitment appeared. Some swore by heaven, others by earth. Some by Jerusalem, some by the temple, some even by their own head.

But behind all these variations was a system of legalistic wiggle room. If you swore by something "less sacred," you had an out. If you didn't use the actual Name of God, your vow might not be binding. It was a kind of spiritual fraud—words dressed in religious garb to give an illusion of gravity without true accountability.

Jesus exposed it all.

"Swear not at all…"

Why?

Because the entire system had become a mockery of truth.

Because every part of creation belongs to God.

Because no man has the authority to manipulate God's Name to protect his own unreliability.

Jesus wasn't just reforming speech.

He was cleansing the temple of language.

II. The Throne, the Footstool, and the City

Jesus points to three specific things often used in oaths: Heaven, Earth, and Jerusalem.

Each had spiritual weight to the Jewish mind:
- Heaven was the dwelling place of God.
- Earth was where God's purposes were manifested.
- Jerusalem was the city of the great King—David's throne and the center of worship.

But Jesus does not just identify these sacred objects—He reclaims them.
- Heaven is God's throne.
- Earth is His footstool.
- Jerusalem belongs to the Great King—not the Sanhedrin.
- In other words, you don't get to borrow divine things to boost your human credibility.

You are not the owner.

You are a steward.

A witness.

A dust-made soul carrying breath not your own.

To use God's creation to cover your own spiritual instability is blasphemous—whether you say His actual Name or not.

III. The Illusion of Control

Jesus adds another startling line:

> "Do not swear by your own head, because you cannot make even one hair white or black."

This is more than poetic commentary on aging. It is a theological blow to the ego.

You don't control anything.

Not your breath.

Not your lifespan.

Not your own hair color—not truly, not permanently.

So why pretend you can guarantee the future with your own words?

Oaths, in this context, were often expressions of self-willed control. A way of declaring, "I swear on my life," as if your life was yours to bargain with.

But Jesus sees through it.

He exposes the truth we try to avoid:

We are not sovereign.

Only God is.

Therefore, any vow made apart from Him is a lie—because it assumes power we do not possess.

IV. The Holy Danger of Using God's Name

While Jesus is targeting false oaths, He is also safeguarding something infinitely more precious:

The holiness of God's Name.

In Jewish tradition, the Divine Name—YHWH—was so sacred it was not even spoken aloud. It was veiled, protected, referenced indirectly to avoid misuse. The Third Commandment was taken with utmost seriousness:

"Thou shalt not take the name of the Lord thy God in vain..."
(Exodus 20:7)

But the Pharisees had found a way around it—invoking holy things without invoking God directly.

And so they swore by heaven. By Jerusalem. By the temple.

Jesus unveils the absurdity:

"You're still invoking the Creator. You're still misusing what belongs to Him."

The Name of God is not a tool to make our promises seem holy.

It is not a verbal spice to flavor our commitments.

It is a consuming fire, not to be handled casually.

If we misuse the Name, we don't just stain our speech—we misrepresent His nature.

V. Let the Words Be Few but True

This command of Jesus is not anti-promise. It is anti-performance.

He is not condemning sacred covenants made in reverence (like marriage, ordination, or dedication).

He is confronting the human tendency to over-speak and under-live.

Words were never meant to be decorations.

They are meant to be mirrors of the heart.

And in the Kingdom of Heaven, a simple "yes" from a holy person carries more weight than a thousand vows from an unstable one.

That's why Jesus says:

"Let your communication be, Yea, yea; Nay, nay."

In Hebrew and Aramaic thought, repetition adds weight:

Yes, yes. No, no.

It is not empty emphasis—it is certainty.

It is how truth walks.

The disciple of Jesus should be known not by their charisma, but by their consistency.

Their word should be so clean, so dependable, that no oath is needed to prove it.

VI. Vows in the Secret Place

But what of sacred vows—those made not to impress, but in moments of holy surrender?

The Bible is not silent.

Ecclesiastes warns:

"When thou vowest a vow unto God, defer not to pay it...

Better is it that thou shouldest not vow, than that thou shouldest vow and not pay." (Ecclesiastes 5:4–5)

This is the vow of Hannah, who gave her son Samuel to the Lord.

The Nazarite vow of separation.

The vow of consecration and calling.

These vows are not forbidden—they are feared.

They are not evil—they are eternal in their consequence.

Jesus is not against sacred covenant.

He is against using God's name in frivolous, selfish, or manipulative ways.

If you vow—mean it.

If you promise—keep it.

If you speak—speak with the weight of the Spirit behind your words.

VII. A Life That Needs No Oaths

In the end, the best vow is not spoken—it is lived. The life of a Kingdom disciple is a constant "yes" to the Lord and a firm "no" to compromise.

It does not rely on oaths.

It does not seek applause.

It walks in the quiet strength of truth.

Let others speak in riddles.

Let others posture with elaborate promises.

You—walk plainly.

Speak truthfully.

Let your word be an echo of your integrity.

Jesus doesn't need your performance.

He wants your purity.

VIII. Conclusion: Words That Smell Like Heaven

We live in a world of spin, slogans, and religious noise.

But the Bride of Christ must sound different.

Her "yes" must be holy.

Her "no" must be rooted in courage.

Her speech must carry the aroma of Heaven.

No embellishment. No spiritual manipulation. No misuse of sacred things.

The mouth is not a stage. It is a sanctuary.

Let the Name of God be honored—not used.

Swear not at all.

Let your life speak louder than your lips.

And let every word you speak reflect the One whose Word became flesh.

Chapter III
The Secret Life
— When No One Is Watching

"Take heed that ye do not your alms before men, to be seen of them: otherwise ye have no reward of your Father which is in heaven. Therefore when thou doest thine alms, do not sound a trumpet before thee, as the hypocrites do... that they may have glory of men... But when thou doest alms, let not thy left hand know what thy right hand doeth... And thy Father which seeth in secret Himself shall reward thee openly."

— Matthew 6:1–4 (KJV)

There are places in the spirit where only God can go.

Rooms of the heart so deep that even our closest companions cannot enter.

Motives that only the Creator sees.

Thoughts that pass like shadows across the soul, invisible to the eye but visible to Heaven.

It is here—in the secret place—that Jesus now turns His attention.

The mountain does not only call us higher; it calls us inward.

Not toward the crowd, but away from it.

Not into performance, but into purity.

Not toward applause, but into the solitary silence where God watches in full light.

I. The Unseen Stage

Jesus begins with a warning:

"Take heed…"

It is a caution to the soul.

Not about the dangers of external sin—but about the hidden poison of religious performance.

The temptation is subtle:

To do good—but to do it with the wrong audience in mind.

To serve—but to seek being seen.

To give—but to crave recognition.

To appear holy—yet inwardly hollow.

The warning is not about generosity, prayer, or fasting.

It is about motive.

A spiritual cancer that turns acts of devotion into acts of self-worship.

II. The Hypocrite's Trumpet

"Do not sound a trumpet before thee, as the hypocrites do…"

The hypocrite does not always lie with his words.

He lies with his intent.

In the first century, religious leaders were known to give alms in public squares, drop coins into temple boxes with loud clatter, and pray in conspicuous locations—making sure all saw their piety. Their good deeds became theater. Their virtue became a show with lighting and sound effects.

Jesus calls it what it is: hypocrisy.

The Greek word hypokritēs means actor—one who wears a mask.

They may speak truth, but they use truth as costume, not as covenant.

And what is their reward?

> "They have their reward."

They wanted attention. They got it.

> But Heaven is silent.

III. The Left Hand Must Not Know

In the Kingdom of Heaven, the purest acts are the quietest.

Jesus says:

> "When you give, let not your left hand know what your right hand is doing."

It is not a call to secrecy for secrecy's sake.

It is an invitation into a realm where only God sees, and that's enough.

The image is profound:

> One hand moving in generosity while the other remains ignorant.
>
> Not even the self should boast.

This is what true holiness looks like:

> Not the suppression of action, but the surrender of recognition.
>
> If your giving must be seen to feel real,
>
> if your praying needs validation,
>
> if your fasting must be advertised,
>
> then your treasure is on earth—and it is already spent.

But if you can give, pray, fast, and love in silence, you have entered the life of the secret place and there, the Father walks.

IV. The Father Who Sees in Secret

These are the most tender words in the Sermon:

> "Thy Father which seeth in secret…"

He sees what no one else notices:
- The gift given anonymously.
- The tear shed in silence.
- The prayer whispered in the dark.
- The sin resisted when no one would know otherwise.

God is not merely the Judge of external acts.

He is the Lover of inward truth.

He does not ask for performance.

He asks for presence.

In the secret place, you are not applauded—you are known.

You are not evaluated—you are searched and loved.

V. The Currency of Heaven

In this secret economy, reward is not applause.

It is not promotion.

It is not earthly gain.

The reward is God Himself.

Those who live for the secret place do not trade in human currency.

They seek intimacy. Nearness. Truth. Transformation.

And in time, the outward will be touched by the inward.

Jesus says:

"…thy Father which seeth in secret shall reward thee openly."

Not in the way of the world—but in divine timing and divine ways.

Open reward does not mean a spotlight.

It means evidence: fruit that only Heaven could have grown.

Peace no one can steal.

Wisdom that no book taught.

Favor that no man orchestrated.

VI. The Secret Place Is the Furnace

It is in the secret that fire purifies.

When no one is watching,

we confront the idols we thought we had destroyed.

We hear the echo of our own voices in prayer—and wonder if we believe what we're saying.

We wrestle. We weep.

We become real.

This is the furnace of authenticity.

Where flesh dies and spirit rises.

Where masks burn and mercy builds.

And it is the only place where true discipleship is born.

VII. Public Ministry vs. Private Holiness

Many want the stage. Few want the solitude.

Many want power. Few want purity.

Many want anointing. Few want alignment.

But Jesus was always retreating to mountains and gardens.

He woke before dawn. He disappeared into wildernesses.

Not to escape the crowd—but to escape self-reliance.

He modeled the secret life.

A life grounded in communion, not performance.

In presence, not popularity.

In prayer, not applause.

So must it be with us.

The secret life is not optional.

It is the foundation of all Kingdom power.

VIII. What You Do When No One Is Watching

This is the test of who you are:

- What do you do when there's no camera?
- What do you think when the platform disappears?
- How do you speak when the door is closed?
- Do you still give, still pray, still fast—without recognition?

Because if you do, you are not playing religion—you are becoming like Jesus.

Holiness is not proven in the sanctuary, but in the hallway.

In the kitchen.

In the moments between.

Character is forged where no praise is heard.

IX. Conclusion: From Hidden to Holy

Jesus did not say, "Be seen."

He said, "Be holy."

He did not say, "Be loud."

He said, "Be faithful."

He did not say, "Be validated."

He said, "Be unseen—and be satisfied."

The secret life is not glamorous.

It is sacred.

And in the final judgment, what was done in secret will not only be rewarded—it will be revealed.

So, enter your chamber.

Shut the door.

Speak to your Father.

And live a life that needs no trumpet, no stage, no signature—just His smile.

That is reward enough.

Chapter IV
When You Pray
— Enter Into Thy Closet

"But thou, when thou prayest, enter into thy closet, and when thou hast shut thy door, pray to thy Father which is in secret; and thy Father which seeth in secret shall reward thee openly."

— Matthew 6:6 (KJV)

There is a place in the Spirit where words become whispers, and whispers become worship.

It is not found in the temple courts.

Not at the synagogue steps.

Not in the noisy corners of public ministry.

It is in the closet.

A door. A silence. A soul. A Father.

Jesus invites us into this room—not to isolate us from reality, but to draw us deeper into the reality that matters most: communion with the unseen God.

In this single verse, Jesus speaks to the architecture of prayer. Not its formula, but its location—both physically and spiritually.

I. Not If You Pray, But When

Notice His language:

"When you pray…"

Not if, but when.

Prayer is not optional in the life of the disciple.

It is not a supplement to spiritual life—it is the spiritual life.

To follow Jesus is to become someone who prays.

To truly love the Lord is to speak to Him, and hear Him speak back.

Yet Jesus doesn't begin by teaching what to say.

He begins with where to go.

Because before you say anything, you must leave something—the stage, the crowd, the pressure to perform.

II. Enter Your Closet

"Enter into thy closet…"

The Greek word used here for "closet" is ταμεῖον (tameion)—literally, a private storeroom or inner chamber.

It is the place of hiding, of quiet, of undistracted presence.

In Hebrew thought, it echoes the inner room of the house—sometimes even the bedroom, or the most intimate dwelling.

The message is clear:

    Go alone.

    Go honestly.

    Go inward.

The closet is not about the walls—it is about the separation.

From noise. From image. From validation. From applause.

There, stripped of all pretense, you meet the only One who matters.

III. Shut the Door

"…and when thou hast shut thy door…"

The shutting of the door is both literal and symbolic.

It is the boundary between outer chaos and inner peace.

It is a declaration: Nothing comes in here but God.

To shut the door is to silence:
- The opinions of people
- The notifications of devices
- The echo of self-doubt
- The nagging demands of productivity

It is to make space where only one Voice is allowed to speak.

Many people pray without ever shutting the door.

They carry the crowd into their solitude.

They pray with their lips but perform in their minds.

But Jesus is specific: shut it.

Seal it.

Turn the lock.

Not to trap yourself, but to free your soul.

IV. To Thy Father Which Is in Secret

"…pray to thy Father which is in secret…"

Here is the miracle:

God is waiting in the secret place.

He is not just on the mountain.

Not just in the fire.

Not just in the cloud.

He is in secret.

He is not accessed through ritual but through reverence.

He is not discovered through spectacle but through stillness.

The God who spoke the universe into being now listens for your voice—not in public declarations, but in private surrender.

There is no audience here.

No competition.

No branding.

No echo but His.

He is already there—waiting.

V. What the Closet Teaches

The closet becomes a school of the Spirit.

It teaches:

- Humility, because no one is watching
- Clarity, because the noise is gone
- Honesty, because masks fall off
- Depth, because there is time to linger
- Reverence, because the Presence is real

You learn that prayer is not performance.

It is not about sounding holy.

It is not about feeling eloquent.

It is about being true—with God, with yourself, with your longings, your failures, your hopes.

You go into the closet empty.

You come out filled.

Not with answers, always—but with awareness.

VI. The Reward That Comes

"…thy Father which seeth in secret shall reward thee openly."

The promise is breathtaking.

God doesn't just see—He responds.

But the reward is not always money, miracles, or success.

Sometimes the reward is:

- Peace that surpasses understanding
- Strength to endure the storm
- Wisdom to make holy decisions

- Healing of the heart, not just the body
- God's presence resting on you like oil

Prayer is not a transaction.

It is a transfer of trust.

You do not manipulate God.

You meet Him.

And when you do, the fruit of that meeting shows up in public.

Others will see joy in your eyes that wasn't there before.

Patience in your reactions.

Glory in your silence.

Power in your weakness.

That is the open reward.

VII. Prayer Without Applause

Jesus' teaching is a rebuke to performance-driven religion.

He had already said:

> *"Do not be like the hypocrites, for they love to pray standing in the synagogues and on the corners of the streets, that they may be seen of men." (Matthew 6:5)*

That was the norm—public prayers for public credit.

Long-winded petitions. Spiritualized speeches. Loud piety to gain reputation.

But God is not impressed.

He waits not on the street corners, but in the secret chamber.

And those who truly know Him, know that's where the fire falls.

VIII. The Closet Is the Upper Room

Every revival began in a room.

- The Upper Room in Acts 1: a closet of 120 souls.
- Elijah's chamber, where he lay the dead boy and cried to God.
- Daniel's window, facing Jerusalem in solitude.
- Jesus Himself, praying all night alone before choosing the twelve.

The world was changed not by conferences, but by closets.

Because prayer is the seed of power.

The closet is where the Spirit broods.

It is where burdens are birthed, strategies are revealed, and strength is made perfect in weakness.

The one who knows the secret place becomes a friend of God.

IX. What Keeps Us from the Closet?

Many things.

- Pride, that prefers public ministry over private intimacy
- Fear, that avoids the silence where our true selves surface
- Busyness, that treats prayer as optional rather than essential
- Guilt, that believes God won't receive us unless we're perfect
- But all of these are lies.

And Jesus demolishes them with a single invitation:

"Enter…"

He does not say, "Be worthy first."

He does not say, "Perfect your theology."

He simply says: Enter.

Come as you are. Shut the door. Speak.

He is waiting.

X. Conclusion: The Door Is Still Open

The mountain still speaks, but now the voice moves inward.

He calls you not to a performance, but to a place.

A place where truth is safe.

A place where wounds are washed.

A place where Heaven touches earth in silence.

Enter your closet.

Close the door.

Leave the world outside.

And let God be Father again.

Not just the Creator of galaxies,

but the Listener of your groanings,

the Keeper of your secrets,

the Rewarder of your waiting.

Let every other voice be hushed.

Let the inner chamber be lit by unseen fire.

Let your prayer be real—

And let Heaven answer openly.

Chapter V
Vain Repetitions
— When Prayer Becomes Noise

"But when ye pray, use not vain repetitions, as the heathen do: for they think that they shall be heard for their much speaking. Be not ye therefore like unto them: for your Father knoweth what things ye have need of, before ye ask him."
 — *Matthew 6:7–8 (KJV)*

There is a kind of prayer that reaches Heaven like incense.

And there is another that evaporates into the air—empty words, never touching the heart of God.

Jesus draws a line between them. Not by volume. Not by length.

But by intention.

"Use not vain repetitions…"

These are not the repetitions of the soul groaning, nor the tearful prayers of a persevering heart.

These are hollow mantras, mechanical phrases, religious routines without relationship.

The mountain shakes again—not because prayer is being discouraged, but because it is being purified.

I. The Illusion of Being Heard

"…for they think that they shall be heard for their much speaking."

Jesus is exposing the lie that quantity equals power.

That longer prayers are more effective.

That more words mean more intimacy.

This was common in pagan religions:

- Repeating names of deities in long chants
- Using formulas to manipulate gods
- Believing their deities were distant and needed to be awakened or appeased

But YHWH is not Baal.

And the God of Abraham does not sleep.

"Your Father already knows what you need before you ask."

This changes everything.

Prayer, then, is not a transaction.

It is not a negotiation.

It is not the wearing down of a reluctant deity.

It is communion with a Father who already sees, already cares, already provides.

II. What Are Vain Repetitions?

Vain repetitions are not measured by words, but by emptiness.

A phrase is not vain because it is repeated.

It is vain because it lacks meaning. Heart. Reverence. Sincerity.

Examples of vain repetition include:
- Praying without thinking
- Quoting memorized lines without affection
- Speaking words to impress others in the room
- Attempting to "sound" spiritual while the heart is distant
- Praying more to fill space than to meet God

The problem isn't the repetition.

It's the vanity behind it.

Jesus Himself repeated prayers—three times in Gethsemane.

David cried, "How long, O Lord?" again and again in the Psalms.

The early church continued in "steadfast prayer."

But their repetition was born of burden, not boredom.

Of brokenness, not bravado.

III. The Danger of Religious Noise

Religion has always been tempted to replace intimacy with volume.

Loudness for the sake of sounding powerful.

Formulas to create a sense of control.

Scripts that require no presence of mind or Spirit.

But God is not moved by noise.

He is moved by truth in the inward parts.

> *The Lord is in His holy temple: let all the earth keep silence before Him." (Habakkuk 2:20)*

> *"Be still, and know that I am God." (Psalm 46:10)*

Sometimes the most powerful prayer is not the longest.

It is the one where every word has weight.

IV. The Heart of the Heathen

"As the heathen do…"

The word "heathen" here refers to Gentile pagans—those who did not know the covenant God of Israel.

Their gods were idols—mute, indifferent, unknowable.

So they shouted.

Repeated themselves.

Carved their flesh to prove devotion.

Built altars of noise to gain a response.

It was desperate, empty religion.

But the child of God is not like this.

He does not pray to be seen.

He prays because he is already known.

We don't beg our Father to notice us.

We come boldly to His throne because we are His.

V. Your Father Knows

This is the truth that silences spiritual striving:

"Your Father knoweth what things ye have need of, before ye ask Him."

Why, then, should we ask?

Not to inform Him.

But to involve Him.

Not to notify, but to align.

Prayer is not for God's sake.

It is for ours.

It reminds us who we are.

It reorients us to His will.

It unclutters our hearts.

It trains us to trust, to wait, to obey, to listen.

You are not praying to persuade God to be good.

You are praying to place yourself in the flow of His goodness.

VI. The Prayer That Pleases Heaven

If God already knows, then what kind of prayer pleases Him?

- Sincere prayer, where the heart is unveiled
- Simple prayer, without embellishment or theater
- Bold prayer, rooted in identity as a child
- Worshipful prayer, where He is adored, not used
- Listening prayer, where silence is as sacred as speech

The disciples never asked, "Teach us how to heal," or "Teach us how to lead."

They asked:

> *"Lord, teach us to pray." (Luke 11:1)*

Because in the secret, honest place of prayer, they saw Jesus as He truly was—the Son in communion with the Father.

VII. Empty Words vs. Living Words

The difference between empty and living prayer is not volume—it is presence.

An empty prayer can last 30 minutes and never touch Heaven.

A living prayer can last 30 seconds and shake eternity.

> *"God is Spirit, and those who worship Him must worship in spirit and in truth." (John 4:24)*

Not in hype. Not in tradition.

In spirit—from the depths of the inner man.

And in truth—without mask, without agenda.

The prayer God receives is the one born of the Spirit and bathed in truth.

VIII. Application: How Then Should We Pray?

Jesus will teach this in the next passage—The Lord's Prayer.

But even before that, He gives the groundwork:

1. Pray to the Father, not to impress people.
2. Pray in secret, not on stage.
3. Pray sincerely, not with formulas.
4. Pray as a child, not as a beggar.
5. Pray knowing He hears, not hoping He might.

Prayer is not the key to getting things.

Prayer is the key to being with God.

IX. Conclusion: Silence Is Sometimes the Holiest Sound

When you pray, be honest.

Be quiet if needed.

Be few in words—but full in heart.

Don't repeat to sound strong.

Don't speak to fill air.

Don't manipulate Heaven with spiritual noise.

Let your prayer be a window, not a wall.

Let your words be few, but faithful.

And let your Father hear not your eloquence, but your essence.

Because He already knows.

And He is already near.

Chapter VI
Our Father in Heaven — The Opening of the Pattern

"After this manner therefore pray ye: Our Father which art in heaven, Hallowed be Thy name."
— *Matthew 6:9 (KJV)*

There is no higher prayer than the one taught by the Word Himself.
It is not long.
It is not poetic in the classical sense.
But it is divine in proportion, perfect in posture, and unshakable in revelation.
The Lord's Prayer is not merely a liturgical memory—it is a blueprint.
Each word is a foundation stone.
Each phrase, a doorway into the heart of God.
Each line, a mirror held to the soul of the disciple.
But before the petitions, before the requests for bread and forgiveness and deliverance, there is the opening line:
   "Our Father which art in heaven, hallowed be Thy name."
This is not an introduction.
It is a positioning.

A placing of the soul before the throne.

A recognition of where we begin—in relationship, in reverence, and in right order.

I. After This Manner

Jesus does not say, "Recite these exact words."

He says, "After this manner…"

He offers a model—not a mantra.

A structure, not a script.

The danger of reducing this prayer to repetition is that it becomes what Jesus just warned against: vain repetition.

But to follow its spiritual architecture is to step into a rhythm that leads to the heart of the Father.

Before asking for anything—Jesus teaches us to start with God Himself.

This is the secret of the mountain life:

We pray not because we are desperate for things, but because we are anchored in Someone.

II. Our Father

Two words that change everything:

> Our Father.
>
> Not "the distant Judge."
>
> Not "the cosmic power."
>
> Not "the unknown deity."

Father.

This was revolutionary.

In Jewish tradition, God's name was so holy it could not be pronounced aloud.

He was Adonai, El Shaddai, Elohim—majestic, exalted, above.

But now Jesus—Son of God—says to ordinary people:

> "When you pray, say Our Father…"

He invites us into His relationship.

He opens a door that religion had long kept closed.

He is not just God—He is Abba.

And you are not just a servant—you are a child.

III. The Power of "Our"

The prayer doesn't begin with "My Father."

It begins with Our Father.

This instantly destroys isolation, pride, and superiority.

We are not only children.

We are part of a family.

We kneel with others—redeemed, forgiven, in process, beloved.

You cannot pray rightly if you pray selfishly.

To say "Our Father" is to stand shoulder to shoulder with the rich and poor, the weak and strong, the known and unknown.

In those two words—Our Father—the Kingdom is revealed.

IV. Who Art in Heaven

"…which art in heaven…"

God is near, but He is not common.

He is Father, but He is Majestic.

He is Abba, but He is also the One enthroned above the circle of the earth.

To say "in heaven" is to recognize that our Father is sovereign, holy, other.

He sees the beginning and the end.

He rules over kings, nations, galaxies.

This balances the nearness of "Father" with the transcendence of "Heaven."

The prayer begins not in the dirt, but in the divine seat of authority.

When you say these words, you lift your soul above your circumstances.

You remember that your Father is not bound by your limitations.

He is above all.

V. Hallowed Be Thy Name

This is not a request.

It is an adoration. A reverent cry. A sacred recognition.

"Hallowed be Thy name."

To "hallow" means to make holy, to revere, to set apart, to worship.

The Name of God is not casual.

It is not a footnote.

It is not seasoning for our sentences.

It is the Name by which the dead rise, demons flee, hearts are saved, and kingdoms fall.

To begin prayer with "Hallowed be Thy name" is to cleanse the atmosphere—to burn away the noise of the world and welcome the fear of the Lord.

It is to say:

"Before I ask, I adore."

"Before I cry out, I bow down."

"Before I plead, I praise."

This is the secret of strength: worship before warfare.

VI. Why the Name Matters

In biblical thought, a name is not just a label.

It is an identity, a reputation, a revelation.

To hallow the Name is to remember:

- He is Jehovah Jireh — the Lord Who Provides
- He is El Elyon — God Most High
- He is Jehovah Rapha — the Lord Who Heals
- He is Adonai — Master
- He is El Shaddai — Almighty
- He is YHWH — I Am That I Am
- He is Father, Son, and Spirit — Three in One

When you hallow His Name, you don't make it more holy—

You make your heart more aware of His holiness.

VII. Prayer Begins with Worship

Many treat prayer as a shopping list.

But Jesus teaches that true prayer begins with worship, not wants.

Before you say,

    "Give us this day…"

You must say,

    "Hallowed be Thy Name."

Why?

Because worship aligns the heart.

Worship reorients the soul.

Worship reminds you who He is—and who you are not.

In the secret place, hallowing His Name shifts the atmosphere.

It silences fear.

It subdues flesh.

It sanctifies the soul.

VIII. When the Name Is Defiled

In a world that mocks God,

uses His Name casually,

mixes it with politics,

profanes it on screens and stages—

The disciple must be different.

To say "Hallowed be Thy Name" is to join the angels who cry "Holy, holy, holy."

It is to declare: "Your Name is not for entertainment. It is for exaltation."

The Bride does not speak of her Groom without awe.

She trembles with joy at His Name.

She wears it with reverence.

She guards it in her mouth and in her witness.

IX. The Name Is a Place of Safety

"The name of the LORD is a strong tower: the righteous runneth into it, and is safe." (Proverbs 18:10)

To begin your prayer with His Name is to run into that tower.

Before the war starts.

Before the trial hits.

Before the anxiety rises.

You step into the Name and shut the gates behind you.

You say:

"I don't begin this prayer on earth—I begin it in Heaven."

"I don't come as a beggar—I come as a son."

"I don't lead with my needs—I lead with Your greatness."

X. Conclusion: Begin Where He Is

Every prayer begins in one of two places:

- Either in our condition
- Or in His glory

Jesus teaches us to begin where He is.

Our Father

In Heaven

Hallowed be Thy Name

This is not poetry. It is position.

And if you begin here, you will pray differently.

You will ask without anxiety.

You will worship without hurry.

You will rest—even before the answer comes.

Because the mountain still speaks:

"Start with God. Stay with God.

And end with God—whose Name is holy, and whose mercy never ends."

"The way is narrow... but it leads to light." — Matthew 7:14

Chapter VII
Thy Kingdom Come
— Longing for the Reign of Heaven

"Thy kingdom come. Thy will be done in earth, as it is in heaven."

— *Matthew 6:10 (KJV)*

There is a prayer so bold, so dangerous, and yet so holy, that when it is uttered from the heart, it changes the world:

"Thy Kingdom come."

It is not a request for comfort.

It is not a poetic phrase.

It is the cry of the surrendered. The anthem of the Bride. The groan of the Spirit.

This line is not passive—it is invasion.

To say "Thy Kingdom come" is to invite a complete reversal of earthly order. It is to declare war on selfishness, corruption, and every system built on rebellion against God.

I. What Is the Kingdom?

Before we can pray Thy Kingdom come, we must know what the Kingdom is.

The Kingdom is not just Heaven after death.

It is the active reign of God wherever His will is obeyed.

The Kingdom is:

- Where the poor in spirit are honored
- Where mercy triumphs over judgment
- Where the last are made first
- Where the meek inherit the earth
- Where love governs, truth reigns, and peace flows like a river

The Kingdom is the rule of Christ—not just in government, but in hearts, homes, cities, and nations.

It is both now and not yet.

It is within us, among us, and ultimately coming in fullness when the King returns.

II. This Is a Dangerous Prayer

To pray Thy Kingdom come is to invite God to undo everything we've built without Him.

It is not a request for blessing.

It is a call for surrender.

It says:

- Let my plans die.
- Let my comforts be disturbed.
- Let my will be broken.
- Let Heaven set the agenda—not me.

This prayer wrecks empires.

It topples idols.

It puts flesh to death.

That's why few truly pray it.

And even fewer understand it.

But this is where revival begins.

III. The Kingdom Is a Government

Isaiah prophesied:

> *"The government shall be upon His shoulder..." (Isaiah 9:6)*

This means Jesus does not come merely to inspire—He comes to govern.

He does not ask for our vote.

He does not campaign.

He reigns.

To say Thy Kingdom come is to invite divine government into:

- My thought life
- My relationships
- My finances
- My dreams
- My politics
- My ministry
- My motives

Wherever the King is obeyed, there the Kingdom is.

IV. A Clash of Kingdoms

To pray Thy Kingdom come is to declare war on the kingdoms of this world:

- The kingdom of ego
- The kingdom of pride
- The kingdom of entertainment
- The kingdom of consumerism
- The kingdom of fear
- The kingdom of man-made religion

This is not metaphor.

It is spiritual battle.

Jesus said,

> *"If I by the finger of God cast out devils, no doubt the Kingdom of God is come upon you." (Luke 11:20)*

When the Kingdom comes:

- Demons flee
- Lies collapse
- Justice rises
- The weak are restored
- And the reign of righteousness begins

That is why the enemy hates this prayer.

Because it is a cry for holy takeover.

V. "Thy Will Be Done"

The second half of the verse interprets the first:

"Thy will be done in earth, as it is in heaven."

This is what the Kingdom looks like—God's will on earth.

- Not man's schemes.
- Not religious traditions.
- Not political manipulations.
- God's will—pure, holy, unshakable.

This part of the prayer crushes human pride.

It says:

"Not my will, but Thine be done."

"Not my way, not my timeline, not my comfort."

It is Gethsemane language.

It is Cross-shaped faith.

It is love that trusts even when the path leads to pain.

VI. On Earth as It Is in Heaven

What does Heaven look like?

- No rebellion
- No confusion
- No corruption
- No delay in obedience
- No half-hearted worship

To pray "on earth as it is in heaven" is to ask for a culture shift.

That my house would look like Heaven.

That my heart would respond like the angels.

That my city would echo the righteousness of the throne.

This is not utopian fantasy.

It is the beginning of spiritual reality.

Wherever the Church lives by this prayer, revival follows.

Wherever believers stop playing church and start welcoming the reign of Christ, transformation erupts.

VII. The Kingdom Within

Jesus said:

"The Kingdom of God is within you." (Luke 17:21)

Before the Kingdom overtakes the world, it must overtake me.

- Does He rule my thoughts?
- My affections?
- My time?
- My ambitions?

This is not about religious behavior.

This is about who sits on the throne of the inner life.

When you say Thy Kingdom come, you're saying:

"Start here. Start in me."

VIII. A Cry for the Return

This prayer is also eschatological.

It looks forward to the day when the King returns—when every knee bows and every tongue confesses.

"Even so, come, Lord Jesus." *(Revelation 22:20)*

The early Church lived with this longing.

They didn't build empires.

They lived like citizens of another world.

They burned with one cry:

"Thy Kingdom come!"

We must return to this urgency.

The world is not our home.

The politics of man cannot save.

The throne of God will not be shared.

The Bride says: Come.

The Spirit says: Come.

And the Church must pray again: **"Thy Kingdom come."**

IX. Realigning the Soul

When you pray this line, your soul comes into alignment.

- Anxiety bows.
- Confusion clears.
- Bitterness breaks.
- Priorities reorder.

You no longer chase what culture says you need.

You chase the will of the King.

And in that alignment, peace flows like a river.

Because when the Kingdom comes, everything else finds its place.

X. Conclusion: Let It Begin in Me

This prayer is not a slogan.

It is a summons.

- To surrender
- To warfare
- To humility
- To longing
- To alignment

Say it again:

"Thy Kingdom come. Thy will be done."

Let it burn in your bones.

Let it shape your days.

Let it cleanse your speech.

Let it govern your decisions.

And let it be more than words.

Let it be life.

Let the Kingdom come in your home, your prayer closet, your voice, your silence, your obedience.

Because when the Kingdom truly comes—nothing stays the same.

Chapter VIII
Give Us This Day Our Daily Bread — Learning to Depend Again

"Give us this day our daily bread."
— *Matthew 6:11 (KJV)*

The most childlike line in the Lord's Prayer is also one of the most powerful.

It does not sound lofty.

It does not echo with theological grandeur.

But it touches the very core of the Kingdom: dependency on the Father.

"Give us this day our daily bread."

It is a request.

But deeper still, it is a revelation—that God is not only Creator and King, but Provider, and that we are not only citizens of His Kingdom, but children in need of Him every single day.

I. A Prayer of Simplicity

Notice the tone:

> There is no drama.
>
> No detailed explanation.
>
> No religious embellishment.

Just a humble plea:

> "Give us... bread."

This is the simplicity of childlike faith.

Not manipulative. Not presumptive.

Just real.

Just human.

Just honest hunger brought before a holy Father.

It reminds us that God is not annoyed by our needs.

He welcomes them.

He is not the god of the self-reliant.

He is the God of the dependent.

II. Bread Is More Than Food

Bread, in the Scriptures, is symbolic.

It represents more than food. It points to:

- Sustenance
- Provision
- Strength for the day
- That which is needed to live

In Hebrew thought, bread (lechem) was central to life itself.

To ask for bread is to ask for all that is necessary to survive and thrive—physically, emotionally, spiritually.

Jesus would later say:

> *"I am the Bread of Life." (John 6:35)*

So this line in the prayer is not simply about the pantry.

It is about the presence of the One who feeds the soul.

III. "Give Us…"

The first word is not "Earn," "Buy," or "Trade."

It is:

"Give."

This is a prayer of grace, not merit.

We do not earn breath.

We do not deserve tomorrow.

We do not control provision.

Everything is gift.

To say "Give us…" is to confess:

"I am not self-made. I am God-fed."

"I do not live by the work of my hands alone, but by the mercy of Heaven."

"Every good thing comes from above." (James 1:17)

This posture is foreign to modern minds.

But it is the only posture the Kingdom honors.

IV. "This Day"

This is not a request for lifetime security.

Not for a five-year plan.

Not for retirement portfolios.

It is a daily prayer for daily needs.

God is a day-by-day provider.

Just as He gave manna in the wilderness—only enough for that day—so too He trains our hearts to trust Him one day at a time.

This teaches:

- Contentment in today
- Trust for tomorrow
- Surrender of control
- Gratitude for what is already in hand

To ask for bread "this day" is to stop worrying about next week—and start worshiping in the now.

V. "Our Daily Bread"

This is not luxury.

Not excess.

Not more than is needed.

It is daily.

Just enough.

The portion appointed.

The grace for this stretch of the journey.

God promises to give you what you need for where you are—not what you might need ten seasons from now.

And that is mercy.

Because too much too soon becomes a curse.

But just enough with Him becomes glory.

VI. The Spirit of the Age Hates This Prayer

Why?

Because this line confronts the idolatry of self-sufficiency.

Modern man says:

- "I provide for myself."
- "I built this."
- "I own my future."
- "I don't need anyone."

But this prayer shatters that pride.

It makes us say:

"I am a receiver."

"I am a child."

"I am daily dependent on a God who never runs dry."

This is freedom, not weakness.

Because to live in dependence on God is to live with peace—knowing your source is unshakable.

VII. It Is a Shared Prayer

Jesus teaches us to say:

"Give us this day our daily bread."

Not just: "Give me mine."

This prayer has no room for selfishness.

It does not say: "I'm fine, forget the rest."

It says: "Feed us all, Lord."

It carries intercession—the concern of the family.

When you pray this, you're also praying for:

- The hungry
- The refugee
- The widow
- The jobless
- The unseen
- The soul who has no spiritual bread

The one who prays rightly always prays with others in mind.

VIII. The Bread of the Word

Jesus said:

"Man shall not live by bread alone, but by every word that proceedeth out of the mouth of God." (Matthew 4:4)

So this prayer is also for revelation.

You are asking:

"Feed me with Your Word today."

"Speak to my spirit."

"Give me fresh understanding, not yesterday's leftovers."

Daily bread is not just in your kitchen—it's in your Bible, your closet, your moments of silence before the Lord.

Every day that passes without that Word is a day starved of Heaven's portion.

IX. God Answers in Many Ways

God may answer this prayer:

- Through a paycheck
- Through an unexpected gift
- Through a Scripture that jumps off the page
- Through manna you didn't expect
- Through people you didn't think would help
- Through your own hands—but not your own doing

But however He answers, it's always Him behind the provision.

That's why Jesus taught us to ask daily.

Because the act of asking keeps us aware that He is the Source, not the system.

X. Conclusion: The Joy of Daily Dependency

There is joy in daily dependency.

- It kills pride
- It strengthens faith
- It deepens worship
- It multiplies gratitude
- It produces peace

Say it again:

"Give us this day our daily bread."

Not because He forgot.

But because we must remember.

Remember that we are dust and breath.

Remember that He is good and near.

Remember that today's strength comes from today's grace.

Let the proud boast in their savings.

Let the world chase tomorrow.

You—child of God—ask your Father.

Every morning.

Every season.

Every breath.

And He will feed you—with what you need, when you need it, and more of Himself than you dared expect.

Chapter IX
Forgive Us Our Debts
— The Humility That Heals

"And forgive us our debts, as we forgive our debtors."
— Matthew 6:12 (KJV)

This line in the Lord's Prayer may be the most revealing, the most costly, and the most misunderstood.

Because to ask for forgiveness is to admit something the world teaches us to avoid:

That we are wrong.

That we are guilty.

That we owe a debt we cannot pay.

But in the Kingdom of Heaven, confession is not weakness.

It is worship.

And forgiveness is not cheap.

It is the currency of the Cross.

Jesus teaches us to pray, not just for strength or provision, but for cleansing—daily, intentionally, humbly.

I. The Word "Debts"

The Greek word here for "debts" (opheilēmata) refers to something legally owed—a moral obligation, a wrong that has left us in deficit.

Jesus is not speaking of finances.

He is speaking of sins—missed marks, broken covenants, hidden pride, secret bitterness.

Some translations render it:

"Forgive us our trespasses…"

Others say:

"Forgive us our sins…"

But the concept remains: We have a debt before God.

We have not lived in perfect holiness.

We are not entitled to mercy.

We are recipients, not claimants.

And that humility is where healing begins.

II. This Is a Daily Prayer

Forgiveness is not a one-time event.

It is a daily rhythm of soul-cleansing.

Even the most faithful disciple still stumbles in thought, word, and motive.

Even Peter, James, and John had to be taught this line—because even apostles sin.

Jesus assumes that we will come back to this line often.

Because the moment we forget our need for mercy, we become dangerous:

- Harsh with others
- Blind to our faults
- Deaf to correction
- Hard-hearted in prayer

But when we say, "Forgive us…", we open the window.

We let the light back in.

We admit: I still need the blood.

III. The Pride That Refuses to Ask

Why do many avoid praying this line?

Because it requires honesty.

To ask for forgiveness is to tear down the mask.

It is to say:

- "I was wrong."
- "I sinned."
- "I failed You again."
- "I need grace—again."

The world teaches self-justification:

- "I made a mistake, but I had a reason."
- "It wasn't that bad."
- "Others do worse."

But the Kingdom teaches repentance without excuse.

Not to be shamed—but to be washed.

IV. Mercy Flows From the Throne

Forgiveness is not a reluctant act on God's part.

It is His delight.

> *"He delighteth in mercy." (Micah 7:18)*
>
> *"If we confess our sins, He is faithful and just to forgive us..."*
> *(1 John 1:9)*

This line in the prayer is not begging—it is believing.

Believing that:

- The blood of Jesus is enough
- The Cross has already made provision
- The Father is eager to restore
- There is no stain He cannot remove

When you say "Forgive us our debts," you are not hoping He might.

You are receiving what He already offered at Calvary.

V. "As We Forgive Our Debtors"

Here lies the weight of the prayer.

Jesus does not let us stop at receiving.

He ties our own forgiveness to the forgiveness we extend.

This is not a legal threat—it is a spiritual truth.

If you have been forgiven much, but refuse to forgive others, you are:
- Denying the Cross
- Hardening your heart
- Blocking the flow of grace
- Choosing bitterness over freedom

"Forgive us… as we forgive…"

That one word—as—is both mirror and measure.

VI. Forgiveness Is a Door

Every time you withhold forgiveness from someone, you are:
- Locking a door
- Damaging your soul
- Inviting torment (see *Matthew 18:34*)

But every time you forgive, you are:
- Releasing healing
- Breaking cycles
- Reflecting Jesus
- Honoring the blood

Forgiveness is not saying, "It didn't matter."

It is saying, "It mattered, but I refuse to be mastered by it."

It is not forgetting—it is choosing freedom over revenge.

VII. What Forgiveness Is Not

To be clear, forgiveness is not:
- Denial of wrong
- Pretending nothing happened
- Accepting abuse
- Ignoring justice

Forgiveness is:
- Releasing the right to punish
- Handing the case over to God
- Letting go of inner poison
- Choosing to bless instead of curse

It is the posture of Christ on the Cross:

"Father, forgive them…"

And we, the forgiven, must echo that cry.

VIII. Learning to Forgive Like Jesus

Jesus didn't wait for apologies.

He forgave while nails pierced His hands.

He didn't base His mercy on behavior.

He based it on the Father's will.

When you pray, "Forgive us… as we forgive…", you are inviting that same Spirit into your life.

You are saying:

"Make me like Jesus."

"Let me remember what He paid."

"Let me give what I could never earn."

This is not easy.

It is cruciform.

But it is the only path to peace.

IX. Healing Through Humility

Forgiveness heals not just relationships—but realigns the heart.

It clears the static in the soul.

It restores tenderness.

It guards your worship.

It purifies your prayers.

Unforgiveness clogs the spiritual arteries.

But repentance and release bring life back into the flow.

If you feel stuck—ask who you have not forgiven.

If you feel cold—ask what you've refused to confess.

Because this prayer is the place where Heaven and healing meet.

X. Conclusion: The Flow of the Cross

Say it slowly:

"Forgive us our debts... as we forgive our debtors."

Let it humble you.

Let it cleanse you.

Let it undo the pride.

Let it soften your soul.

This is not just a sentence—it is a spiritual operation.

It reopens the flow of grace.

It reminds you who you are.

It makes you like the King—whose mercy runs deeper than offense, and whose love has no end.

The mountain still speaks.

And today, it says:

"Be forgiven.

Be clean.

And forgive—as you have been forgiven."

Chapter X
Lead Us Not Into Temptation — The Cry for Protection

"And lead us not into temptation, but deliver us from evil."
— Matthew 6:13 (KJV)

This line in the Lord's Prayer is more than a petition.
It is a confession of weakness, a cry for divine direction, and a humble acknowledgment that we are not as strong as we think.
The one who prays this prayer is not afraid to admit:

"I am prone to wander."

"I am vulnerable to sin."

"I need God to lead me away from danger I may not even see."

Jesus Himself gives this line. Not to paralyze us in fear, but to position us under the protection of the Father—a Shepherd who not only feeds His sheep, but leads them away from the wolf.

I. Lead Us

The prayer begins with guidance.

"Lead us…"

This is a declaration that we are not the guides of our own lives.

It dismantles pride.

It silences the voice of self-reliance.

We are asking:

"Father, take the lead."

"You know the way I cannot see."

"Direct my steps."

"Prevent me from going where my flesh might triumph."

To be led by God is to avoid a thousand unnecessary battles.

II. Not Into Temptation

The phrase may strike the ear strangely:

"Lead us not into temptation…"

Does God lead people into temptation?

The answer is clear in Scripture:

"Let no man say when he is tempted, I am tempted of God… for God cannot be tempted with evil, neither tempteth He any man."

(James 1:13)

Jesus is not implying that the Father would trick us.

He is teaching us to pray:

"Father, steer us clear of testing we are too weak to handle."

"Guide us away from moments where we are prone to fall."

"Rescue us from our blind spots before they destroy us."

This is a prayer of preemptive humility.

III. What Is Temptation?

Temptation is more than lust or obvious sin.

It is any moment of enticement to trust in something or someone other than God.

It can appear as:
- Opportunity without prayer
- Promotion without peace
- Relationship without alignment
- Influence without integrity
- Success without sanctification

Temptation whispers:

"Take the shortcut."

"You deserve this."

"No one will know."

"Just this once."

And that whisper, if not discerned, leads to devastation.

So we pray,

"Lead me away. I may not recognize it until it's too late."

IV. The Need for Discernment

This line is also a request for discernment.

There are doors that look like blessings but lead to bondage.

There are voices that sound like opportunity but carry deception.

There are roads that appear safe but are paved by pride.

We need the Spirit of God to lead us—

Not just through open doors, but around traps.

> *"In all thy ways acknowledge Him, and He shall direct thy paths."*
> *(Proverbs 3:6)*

Jesus is teaching us to live with eyes wide open—not walking in fear, but walking in surrender.

V. Deliver Us From Evil

Now the prayer turns from prevention to protection.

"…but deliver us from evil."

Some translations say:

"…deliver us from the evil one."

Both are valid—and both are needed.

We are praying:

- Protect me from Satan
- Protect me from sin
- Protect me from myself
- Protect me from hidden snares
- Protect me from moments of weakness

This is not paranoia.

It is holy awareness.

We have an enemy—not imagined, not symbolic, but real.

And Jesus equips us with a daily cry for rescue.

VI. Deliverance Is a Daily Grace

We do not outgrow this prayer.

You may memorize Scripture.

You may lead ministry.

You may fast for days.

But the need remains:

"Deliver me, Lord.

I am dust.

I am tempted.

I am vulnerable."

Every day we walk through a battlefield.

Every morning this prayer re-arms the spirit.

It is the helmet. The shield. The cry of the watchman.

"Deliver me again."

VII. The Prayer of the Humble

Pride never prays this line.

Pride says:
- "I can handle it."
- "I know better."
- "I won't fall."
- "It's not that dangerous."

But humility prays:
- "Keep me from what I don't see."
- "Guard my feet from familiar traps."
- "Rescue me before I run too far."
- "Only You can save me."

This is why Jesus teaches this prayer near the end—

Because only those who have truly said "Thy Kingdom come" will now cry:

"Keep me from the kingdom of darkness."

VIII. The Trap of Subtle Evil

Not all evil wears horns.

Sometimes evil looks like:
- Compromise for comfort
- Delay in obedience
- A bitter heart that feels justified
- An identity built on ministry instead of sonship
- A success that slowly erodes the soul

This is why we cry:

"Deliver us…"

Deliver me from what feels right but ends in ruin.

Deliver me from myself.

Deliver me from the traps I've walked into before.

Deliver me from the sin that wears a smile.

IX. Jesus Prayed This Too

In Gethsemane, Jesus said:

> *"Watch and pray, that ye enter not into temptation."*
> (Matthew 26:41)

Even the Son of God instructed His disciples to pray against falling.
And He Himself was led into the wilderness to be tempted—
Not by the Father, but by the Spirit for the purpose of triumph.
He faced temptation so that when we face it, we might say:

> "Lord, You overcame. Now deliver me."

He is not a distant intercessor.
He is our High Priest who sympathizes.

X. Conclusion: The Shepherd Still Leads

"Lead us not into temptation… but deliver us from evil."
This is the cry of the sheep who knows his Shepherd.
It is the voice of one who does not trust his flesh.
It is the daily turning of the heart to the God who knows the path.
Say it every morning:

- "Lead me, Father."
- "Guide my feet."
- "Alert my soul."
- "Protect me from the evil one."
- "Deliver me again."

The mountain still speaks.
And today, it says:

> "Let the humble be guarded.
> Let the wise stay low.
> Let the Bride walk close to the Shepherd—and she will not be overtaken."

I. For Thine Is the Kingdom

The prayer began with "Thy Kingdom come"—and it ends by affirming: "Thine is the Kingdom."

This is certainty.

This is faith speaking after surrender.

This is worship responding to revelation.

No matter what I see on the news—

No matter what shakes the nations—

No matter what I feel in the dark—

The Kingdom still belongs to Him.

And it is not merely a kingdom—it is The Kingdom.

Unrivaled. Unshaken. Unstoppable.

> *"The Lord hath prepared His throne in the heavens; and His Kingdom ruleth over all." (Psalm 103:19)*

This ending is not filler.

It is the climax of clarity—that everything I've prayed is under the reign of the King of Kings.

II. And the Power

Not only does the Kingdom belong to Him—so does the power.

- Power to forgive
- Power to provide
- Power to heal
- Power to deliver
- Power to restore
- Power to sustain

God does not need to borrow strength.

He does not outsource miracles.

He is not waiting to be empowered by our faith.

He is power.

Chapter XI
For Thine Is the Kingdom — The Benediction of Glory

"For Thine is the kingdom, and the power, and the glory, for ever. Amen."
— Matthew 6:13b (KJV)

The final line of the Lord's Prayer is not a request.
It is a proclamation.
It is the resounding "Amen" of Heaven echoing through the surrendered heart.
This doxology—often omitted in modern translations but preserved in the hearts of saints for generations—serves as both a benediction and a battle cry.
It gathers up every previous petition and lifts it into worship.
It says:
> "Every need I've named, every weakness I've admitted, every cry I've groaned—I now place under this truth:
> It's all Yours. All the power. All the authority. All the glory. Forever."

And that means every line of the Lord's Prayer can be answered not because we speak well, but because He reigns with absolute might.

III. And the Glory

If the Kingdom is His territory,

And the power is His ability,

Then the glory is His signature—

His unshared radiance, His fame, His name lifted above all.

To say "Thine is the glory" is to say:

> "Let no one else be praised for what only You can do."

> "Let no flesh boast."

> "Let every miracle point to You."

> "Let my answered prayers become altars of adoration."

Glory is not to be hoarded.

It is to be returned—like a crown laid at His feet.

> *Not unto us, O Lord, not unto us, but unto Thy name give glory."*

(Psalm 115:1)

IV. Forever

This is not a seasonal Kingdom.

It is eternal.

It does not rise and fall with empires.

It does not sway with the politics of man.

It does not end when the prayer ends.

It lasts forever.

That means the One we pray to today will still be worthy tomorrow, and ten billion years from now.

This is the heartbeat of eternity:
- God reigning
- God ruling
- God glorified
- God satisfying the hearts of those who love Him—with no end

Of the increase of His government and peace there shall be no end..." (Isaiah 9:7)

V. Amen

One word.

All-in.

"Amen" is not just a closer.

It is a declaration:

"So be it."

"I believe this."

"I stand on this."

"Let it be done."

It seals the prayer—not in ritual, but in faith.

It declares that this wasn't just a poetic sequence of words.

This was truth spoken from earth to Heaven.

"Amen" means: I've said what must be said.

Now I will live it.

VI. Why This Ending Matters

This ending re-centers the soul.

After asking for:
- Bread
- Mercy
- Protection
- Deliverance

We return to the source of it all:

> The King.
>
> We are not the heroes of our own story.
>
> We are not self-made.
>
> We are not prayer warriors because of how we sound.
>
> We are citizens kneeling before the Throne.

This is where the secret life finds its compass again:

> God's Kingdom.
>
> God's power.
>
> God's glory.
>
> Forever.

VII. The Whole Prayer in Light of This Line

Look back at each line through this lens:

- "Our Father in Heaven…" — Because the Kingdom is Yours
- "Hallowed be Thy Name…" — Because the glory is Yours
- "Thy Kingdom come…" — Because it already belongs to You
- "Give us this day…" — Because the power to provide is Yours
- "Forgive us…" — Because only You have power to pardon
- "Lead us not…" — Because You are the Shepherd
- "Deliver us from evil…" — Because Yours is the victory

This ending is not extra.

It is the summary of every sentence.

The exclamation point.

The bow tying every thread of heavenward longing.

VIII. The Glory of the Hidden Place

Let us remember:

> This entire prayer was taught in the context of the secret place.
>
> Not for stages.
>
> Not for religious performance.

But for sons and daughters who close the door, bow the head, and say:

"Father, I belong to Your Kingdom.

I trust in Your power.

I live for Your glory.

Forever. Amen."

What kind of life would be formed if this was our daily language?

What kind of Church would emerge if this was not just recited—but embodied?

IX. A Life Built on the Amen

When the prayer ends, life begins.

- We go out to forgive, because He is the King.
- We resist temptation, because His is the power.
- We walk humbly, because the glory is His.
- We fear no lack, because the Kingdom has no shortage.
- We pray again tomorrow, because the mercy still flows.

The secret life, the narrow way, the consecrated heart—all find their home in this benediction.

It is the fire that burns in private.

It is the song behind every surrender.

It is the language of those who have seen the King.

X. Conclusion: Still He Reigns

"For Thine is the Kingdom, and the power, and the glory, forever. Amen."

Let these words echo in your spirit.

Let them correct what pride tries to build.

Let them re-center what fear tries to scatter.

Say them every day—until you believe them with your bones.

When the world shakes:

"Thine is the Kingdom."

When your strength runs dry:

    "Thine is the power."

When the enemy lies:

    "Thine is the glory."

When tomorrow feels uncertain:

    "Forever."

And when your voice trembles:

    "Amen."

Chapter XII
The Narrow Way
— Few Find It, but It Leads to Life

"Enter ye in at the strait gate: for wide is the gate, and broad is the way, that leadeth to destruction, and many there be which go in thereat: Because strait is the gate, and narrow is the way, which leadeth unto life, and few there be that find it."

— Matthew 7:13–14 (KJV)

The sermon turns.

The call sharpens.

The invitation narrows.

After a mountain full of blessing, prayer, fasting, forgiveness, and the glory of God—Jesus places before the soul a choice:

Two gates. Two paths. Two destinies.

And with it, a warning:

"Few will find the narrow way."

This is not because God hides it.

It is because the way is costly, and few are willing to pay the price of surrender.

But for those who do, the path may be hard—but it leads to life.

I. The Strait Gate

"Enter ye in at the strait gate…"

"Strait" does not mean crooked. It means tight, compressed, constrained.

The entry into the Kingdom is not wide open to every idea, every doctrine, every compromise.

It is exactly as wide as Christ alone.

You do not squeeze in with your own righteousness.

You cannot bring your idols with you.

You cannot justify half-surrender.

This gate requires you to lay it all down:

- Ego
- Titles
- Bitterness
- Secret sins
- Self-made religion

Jesus is not looking for crowd approval.

He is warning:

"This path begins with a gate that only the broken can walk through."

II. The Broad Way

"…wide is the gate, and broad is the way, that leadeth to destruction…"

The broad way is:

- Popular
- Easy
- Culturally affirmed
- Spiritually vague
- Morally accommodating

It requires no repentance.

No self-denial.

No holiness.

Just movement. Just comfort. Just consensus.

The broad way feels safe because so many walk it.

But Jesus says plainly:

"It leads to destruction."

Destruction of what?

- The soul
- The image of God
- The call on your life
- The fellowship of the Spirit
- The future you were meant to walk in

III. The Narrow Way

"…narrow is the way, which leadeth unto life…"

This is not a path for the lazy or distracted.

It is not a path for the double-minded.

It is narrow because:

- It does not bend to the flesh
- It does not flatter sin
- It does not applaud pride
- It does not compete for attention
- It is carved by the footsteps of the Crucified One

This path is not about restriction—it is about direction.

It is narrow like the veins in the body—because it leads to the heart.

It is narrow like a surgical incision—because it heals what is deep.

IV. Few There Be That Find It

Jesus says this not with glee, but with grief.

"Few there be that find it."

Not because it's hidden—

But because it is rejected.

It requires:
- A turning
- A bowing
- A hunger for righteousness
- A willingness to look foolish to the world
- A radical embrace of the Cross

The Kingdom is open to all—but few choose to lose themselves to enter.

This is not elitism.

It is a spiritual fact.

Broad is the stage. Narrow is the altar.

V. The Way Is a Person

Jesus does not just teach the narrow way—He is the Way.

"I am the way, the truth, and the life..." (John 14:6)

He walked it first:
- Rejected by men
- Obedient to death
- Misunderstood
- Yet full of joy
- Yet full of fire
- Yet full of the Father's pleasure

To walk the narrow way is to follow the Lamb wherever He goes.

Not just in theology, but in daily obedience.

VI. Walking the Way Looks Like…
- Forgiving when it's easier to hate
- Telling the truth when it costs you
- Refusing compromise in secret
- Loving enemies

- Losing arguments to keep peace
- Giving generously
- Living prayerfully
- Choosing holiness over relevance

It is not flashy.

But it is full of fire.

The fire of purity.

The fire of communion.

The fire of love.

VII. The Narrow Way Leads to Life

Not just eternal life later—but abundant life now.

- Peace in the storm
- Clarity in the noise
- Power in the weakness
- Joy that doesn't depend on applause
- Intimacy with the Father

This is not the path of death—it is the path that kills the false self so the real self can breathe.

It is not just hard—it is holy.

And it ends in glory.

> *"Thou wilt shew me the path of life: in Thy presence is fulness of joy..." (Psalm 16:11)*

VIII. The Mountain and the Way

The Sermon began with blessing.

But it ends with decision.

You have heard the words.

You have seen the vision.

You have tasted the truth.

Now: Will you walk?

This is where many turn back.

The crowd listens—but few follow.

Many admire—but few obey.

But the mountain still speaks.

It calls for those willing to say:

> "Even if I must walk alone—
> even if the path is lonely—
> even if it costs me everything—
> I choose the narrow way."

IX. Encouragement for the Few

You may feel outnumbered.

You may feel mocked.

You may feel like the only one still holding the line.

But you are not alone.

- Elijah thought he was alone—but God had 7,000.
- Noah preached righteousness while the world laughed.
- Paul pressed on though forsaken.
- Jesus carried the Cross when no one else could.

You walk a narrow way—but you walk it with angels.

With the saints.

With the Spirit.

With your name written in Heaven.

X. Conclusion: Enter

> "Enter ye in…"

Jesus ends this teaching with a command.

Not a suggestion.

Not a poetic invitation.

A call.

> "Enter."

Don't just admire the way.

Don't just read about the way.

Don't just argue theology about the way.
Walk it.
With trembling joy.
With focused heart.
With holy fear.
Let the world have its broad path.
Let the many find destruction.
But you—child of the mountain—
find the way that leads to life.

Chapter XIII
The Rock That Stands
— Building a Life on Unshakable Ground

"Therefore whosoever heareth these sayings of Mine, and doeth them, I will liken him unto a wise man, which built his house upon a rock: And the rain descended, and the floods came, and the winds blew, and beat upon that house; and it fell not: for it was founded upon a rock. And every one that heareth these sayings of Mine, and doeth them not, shall be likened unto a foolish man, which built his house upon the sand: And the rain descended, and the floods came, and the winds blew, and beat upon that house; and it fell: and great was the fall of it."

— *Matthew 7:24–27 (KJV)*

The sermon ends with a story.

A picture. A parable. A choice.

Jesus has given truths that shake the heavens—

Now He speaks of foundations that hold the soul.

And He makes it plain:

"You've heard what I've said.

The question is: Will you build your life on it?"

I. The Word Therefore

"Therefore whosoever heareth these sayings of Mine…"

The word "therefore" is the hinge of the sermon.

It means: Because of everything you've just heard—about anger, prayer, forgiveness, the narrow way, the Kingdom, the secret life—now this is what must follow.

It is the line between admiration and application.

Between listeners and builders.

Between hearers only, and those who do His will.

The sermon has never been about inspiration.

It has always been about transformation.

II. The Two Builders

Jesus presents two men.

Both are building.

Both are hearing.

Both face storms.

But one stands. One falls.

The difference? Not effort. Not location. Not appearance.

The foundation.

A. The Wise Man

"…built his house upon a rock…"

This is the one who hears and does the Word.

He responds in obedience—not emotion, not delay, not excuses.

He applies the Word in:
- Thought and speech
- Family and finances
- Trials and quiet places
- Marriage, ministry, motives

His life is not perfect. But it is anchored.

He digs deep. He builds slow.

And when the winds come, the households.

Because the foundation is not personality or popularity—it is Christ.

B. The Foolish Man

"…built his house upon the sand…"

He hears the same words.

But he chooses not to obey.
- Perhaps he applauds the sermon.
- Perhaps he even recites it.
- But he does not apply it.

His house may look impressive.

His platform may reach high.

But there are cracks beneath the surface.

And when the rains fall—he discovers

what he built was never real.

"And great was the fall of it…"

III. The Storm Is Certain

Note that both houses face the storm.
- The wise are not spared difficulty.
- The obedient are not exempt from pain.
- But only the house built on truth remains.

Jesus never promised that faith would prevent storms.

He promised that faith built on Him would withstand them.

The storm tests what was hidden.
- It exposes the foundation.
- It reveals what the applause could not.
- It shows whether the soul is anchored in eternity or held up by emotion.

IV. What Does It Mean to Build on the Rock?

It means:
- You take Jesus seriously.
- You obey what He says, even when it's costly.
- You forgive when it hurts.
- You love enemies without applause.
- You give in secret.
- You endure trials without collapsing into self-pity.
- You live for eternity, not attention.

To build on the rock is to make the teachings of Jesus your blueprint for life.

No edits. No dilution. No substitutions.

> *"Be ye doers of the word, and not hearers only, deceiving your own selves." (James 1:22)*

V. The Rock Is a Person

The rock is not just obedience.

The rock is Christ Himself.

> *For other foundation can no man lay than that is laid, which is Jesus Christ." (1 Corinthians 3:11)*

Jesus is the foundation that does not crack.

The truth that does not shift.

The anchor that holds in every age.

He is the Rock struck in the wilderness.

The Stone the builders rejected.

The Cornerstone that aligns the whole structure.

The Refuge that never moves.

To build on the rock is to make Jesus the Lord of all.

VI. What Does It Mean to Fall?

"...and great was the fall of it."

This is not just the fall of a building.

It is the collapse of a life built on half-truths and self-made righteousness.

It is the crash of the untested soul.

It is what happens when religion is admired but not embodied.

The fall can look like:
- A hidden sin exposed
- A public failure
- A private unraveling
- A faith that does not survive grief
- A calling built on charisma, not character

But the warning is mercy.

Jesus tells us this now—so we do not have to collapse later.

VII. The End of the Sermon, the Beginning of the Life

The Sermon on the Mount ends not with a benediction, but with a building site.

He has given the design.

The question is:

Will you build?

Not someday.

Not when life calms down.

Now.

Each decision is a brick.

Each surrender a nail.

Each act of obedience a beam.

Until your house stands—not for a season, but for eternity.

VIII. What It Means Today

If you are reading this and feel the tremble of conviction, do not despair.

This is grace calling you deeper.

You can tear down the faulty foundation.

You can rebuild with Christ.

- Tear down the pride
- Lay aside the shallow doctrine
- Remove the appearance-driven habits
- Return to the secret place
- Build in the Spirit
- Build with trembling
- Build with worship

Except the Lord build the house, they labour in vain that build it..."
(Psalm 127:1)

IX. The Mountain Still Speaks

It speaks still.

Not just in sermons, but in storms.

Not just in the secret place, but in the trials of life.

And it asks:

Will you build what lasts?

Not what impresses.

Not what pleases the crowd.

Not what draws numbers.

But what stands.

X. Conclusion: The Rock or the Sand

You will build.

That is not optional.

But what you build on—that is your choice.
So, choose the Rock.
Choose the truth.
Choose the Lord Jesus—not just as Savior, but as Foundation.
Let the world clap for the sand.
Let the storm come.
But you—child of the mountain—
Build with eternity in view.
And when the flood rises,
when the wind howls,
when the night presses in—
Your house will still be standing.
Because the Rock still holds.

Chapter XIV
The Voice That Amazes — When the Crowd Heard Him

"And it came to pass, when Jesus had ended these sayings, the people were astonished at His doctrine: For He taught them as one having authority, and not as the scribes."
— *Matthew 7:28–29 (KJV)*

The mountain grew still.
The final word had been spoken.
The echo of eternity lingered in the air.
And the people stood—astonished.
Jesus had not shouted.
He had not gestured wildly.
He had not quoted a hundred rabbis.
He had simply spoken—
And the world changed.

I. The Sermon Ends, but the Voice Lingers

The Sermon on the Mount does not end with fireworks.

It ends with authority.

- Not borrowed
- Not speculative
- Not derivative
- Not debated

But originating in Heaven itself.

When He had ended these sayings, the people did not return to their old ways right away.

They were shaken, stirred, arrested by the Voice that had spoken directly to the soul.

The voice of Christ doesn't just speak to the mind.

It summons the conscience.

II. Not as the Scribes

The scribes spoke with education.

Jesus spoke with possession.

- They quoted. He revealed.
- They referenced. He embodied.
- They discussed. He declared.
- They parsed law. He pierced hearts.

His authority was not based on scrolls or schooling.

It was based on the fact that He is the Word made flesh.

"Never man spake like this man." (John 7:46)

This is the Voice that once said,

"Let there be light."

And there was.

And now He speaks again—

"Let there be truth."

And there must be.

III. The Response of the People

"The people were astonished…"

Astonished—because they had never heard truth this pure.

Not dressed up in religion.

Not diluted for popularity.

Not twisted for politics.

But raw. Holy. Cutting. Healing.

They didn't just learn something—

They felt something eternal move inside them.

That's what real truth does.

- It arrests.
- It awakens.
- It reorders.
- It convicts.
- It invites.
- It demands a response.

IV. What Authority Sounds Like

Jesus did not sound authoritative because He was loud—

But because His words matched His life.

- He forgave sinners and preached forgiveness.
- He healed the sick and declared compassion.
- He blessed the poor and lived with nothing.
- He called for the Cross and carried it first.

His voice held weight because His soul held purity.

Authority in the Kingdom is not from position—

It is from submission.

"He humbled Himself…" (Philippians 2:8)

And therefore:

"God hath highly exalted Him…" (Philippians 2:9)

V. The Voice Still Speaks

The mountain may be silent,

but the Voice still speaks.

- Through the Scriptures
- Through the Spirit
- Through the conscience
- Through the pages of His Word
- Through the whispers in the secret place

And still—

It amazes.

It cuts.

It calls.

It restores.

It requires.

VI. How We Must Respond

Some heard and walked away.

Some heard and followed Him.

Some heard and crucified Him.

Some heard and gave everything.

And now we have heard.

What will we do with the Voice?

Will we:

- Study it but not submit to it?
- Admire it but not obey it?
- Quote it but not be changed by it?

Or will we let it undo us and rebuild us?

> *"Today, if ye will hear His voice, harden not your hearts..."*
> *(Hebrews 3:7–8)*

VII. The Mountain Still Speaks

It speaks in 2025 like it did on that Galilean hillside.

- It calls to the prideful and says: Bow.
- It calls to the religious and says: Repent.
- It calls to the weary and says: Come.
- It calls to the hungry and says: Feast.
- It calls to the fearful and says: Stand.

It is not a dead sermon.

It is a living covenant.

> *"Heaven and earth shall pass away, but My words shall not pass away."*
> *(Matthew 24:35)*

The mountain may have been vacated by feet—

But it is still inhabited by fire.

VIII. You Have Heard It Now

You have read the words.

You have seen the contrast between the broad and the narrow.

You have heard the prayer, the call to secrecy, the warnings, the hope.

You have stood where the crowd stood.

The difference now is that you cannot unhear it.

What happens next is not about the preacher.

It is about the hearer.

Will you be:

- A wise builder?
- A kingdom seeker?
- A truth doer?
- A storm survivor?
- A disciple?

IX. Conclusion: The Voice or the Noise?

Many voices compete for attention.

But one still astonishes.

The voice of the Shepherd.

The voice of the King.

The voice of Jesus.

He speaks still—

To the secret life,

To the narrow heart,

To the soul that says yes.

So build your life on what He said.

Let the world scroll and scream.

But you—child of the mountain—

Tremble at His Word.

And stand amazed.

> *"The grass withereth, the flower fadeth: but the word of our God shall stand forever." (Isaiah 40:8)*

"Sacred Stillness and Divine Conclusion"

In the hush of all striving, Heaven descends. When every voice is silenced but the Spirit's, truth is heard. This is the stillness where eternity speaks and glory remains.
DBC

GLOSSARY OF KEY BIBLICAL TERMS

Authority (Biblical)

The divine right and power by which God speaks, commands, and governs. In the context of Jesus 'teachings, authority is not merely positional but intrinsic—it comes from being the eternal Word made flesh. His words are not suggestions; they are sovereign truth.

Closet (Prayer Closet)

A secret, sacred space of solitude where one meets with God in undistracted intimacy. It symbolizes the hidden life of prayer—a place of surrender, honesty, and communion, far from the gaze of men.

Debts (Spiritual)

Symbolic of sins or moral failings owed against the holiness of God. When we pray, "Forgive us our debts," we acknowledge our transgressions and ask for divine pardon. Also reflects the necessity of forgiving others.

The Narrow Way

A metaphor Jesus uses to describe the difficult, disciplined, and often lonely path that leads to life. It stands in contrast to the broad road of ease, popularity, and compromise that leads to destruction.

Secret Life (of the Disciple)

The inner, unseen world of the believer where motives, thoughts, and personal obedience reside. It is the truest test of faith—not what is seen publicly, but what is lived privately before God.

Righteousness

Right standing with God, not achieved by human effort but received by grace through faith and walked out in obedience. In the Sermon on the Mount, righteousness is deeper than law-keeping—it is a transformed heart and life aligned with the holiness of God.

Kingdom of God

God's sovereign reign—both present and future—where His will is done on earth as in heaven. Jesus teaches us to seek first this Kingdom, not as a political regime but as a divine realm of righteousness, peace, and joy in the Holy Spirit.

The Rock

Symbolic of Jesus Christ, the unshakable foundation upon which a life must be built. To build on the rock is to obey His words, trust His character, and withstand the storms of life through divine anchoring.

Temptation

A trial, enticement, or lure to sin—either by the flesh, the world, or the enemy. Jesus teaches us to pray for deliverance from temptation, recognizing our weakness and His strength as the only safeguard.

Forgiveness

The releasing of debt, offense, or accusation toward another, rooted in the forgiveness we ourselves have received from God. It is both a gift and a command, a gateway to freedom and healing.

The Broad Way

The spiritually careless path of the masses—marked by comfort, compromise, and self-will. Though appealing to the flesh, it leads to spiritual ruin. Jesus contrasts it with the narrow way in Matthew 7.

The Voice of the Shepherd

A biblical image drawn from John 10, referring to Jesus as the Good Shepherd whose sheep know His voice. In the context of the Sermon, this voice speaks with clarity, compassion, and authority—and astonishes the soul.

SCRIPTURE INDEX

Genesis
- Genesis 22:8 — Ch. 7

Exodus
- Exodus 16:4 — Ch. 7
- Exodus 20:13–17 — Ch. 2

Leviticus
- Leviticus 19:18 — Ch. 3

Psalm
- Psalm 1:1–3 — Ch. 13
- Psalm 23 — Ch. 9
- Psalm 27:5 — Ch. 10
- Psalm 91:1–2 — Ch. 5
- Psalm 119:11 — Ch. 10
- Psalm 127:1 — Ch. 13
- Psalm 130:3–4 — Ch. 9
- Psalm 139:23–24 — Ch. 5
- Psalm 145:16 — Ch. 7

Proverbs
- Proverbs 3:5–6 — Ch. 10
- Proverbs 4:23 — Ch. 9

Isaiah
- Isaiah 9:6 — Ch. 6
- Isaiah 26:3 — Ch. 10
- Isaiah 40:8 — Ch. 14
- Isaiah 53:5 — Ch. 9
- Isaiah 55:6 — Ch. 14

Jeremiah
- Jeremiah 29:11 — Ch. 6

Ezekiel
- Ezekiel 36:26 — Ch. 9

Matthew
- Matthew 5:3–12 — Ch. 1
- Matthew 5:13–16 — Ch. 2
- Matthew 5:21–26 — Ch. 2
- Matthew 5:27–48 — Ch. 3
- Matthew 6:1–4 — Ch. 4
- Matthew 6:5–6 — Ch. 5
- Matthew 6:7–13 — Ch. 6–11
- Matthew 6:24 — Ch. 6
- Matthew 6:33 — Ch. 6
- Matthew 7:13–14 — Ch. 12
- Matthew 7:24–27 — Ch. 13
- Matthew 7:28–29 — Ch. 14

Mark
- Mark 1:35 — Ch. 5
- Mark 4:24 — Ch. 13

Luke
- Luke 6:46–49 — Ch. 13
- Luke 12:15 — Ch. 6
- Luke 22:42 — Ch. 6

John
- John 1:1 — Ch. 14
- John 6:35 — Ch. 7
- John 7:46 — Ch. 14
- John 10:27 — Ch. 14
- John 13:34–35 — Ch. 3
- John 17:17 — Ch. 14

Acts
- Acts 4:12 — Ch. 13

Romans
- Romans 12:1–2 — Ch. 12

1 Corinthians
- 1 Corinthians 3:11 — Ch. 13
- 1 Corinthians 10:13 — Ch. 10

Galatians
- Galatians 5:22–23 — Ch. 4
- Galatians 6:1 — Ch. 9

Ephesians
- Ephesians 2:8–9 — Ch. 9
- Ephesians 4:32 — Ch. 9
- Ephesians 6:10–18 — Ch. 10

Philippians
- Philippians 2:8–9 — Ch. 14
- Philippians 4:6–7 — Ch. 10

Colossians
- Colossians 3:13 — Ch. 9

Hebrews
- Hebrews 3:7–8 — Ch. 14
- Hebrews 4:12 — Ch. 14
- Hebrews 12:26–27 — Ch. 13

James
- James 1:5 — Ch. 2
- James 1:22 — Ch. 13
- James 3:17 — Ch. 2

1 Peter
- 1 Peter 2:6 — Ch. 13
- 1 Peter 5:8 — Ch. 10

Revelation
- Revelation 3:20 — Ch. 14
- Revelation 21:6–7 — Ch. 13

About the Author

Damiano B. Centola is a visionary writer, theologian, and poetic voice for this generation. With a deep love for Scripture and a reverent command of language, he weaves biblical truth, historical insight, and spiritual fire into every page. His writings echo the eternal and awaken the soul, calling readers not just to believe, but to follow—with heart, mind, and holy surrender.

A student of the Word and a disciple of the Narrow Way, Damiano speaks to the silent spaces of the heart, the sacred longings of the spirit, and the mystery of God revealed in Christ. His works span devotional meditations, theological depth, and prophetic clarity—uniting art and truth in every volume.

He is the author of numerous books, including:
- The Mountain Still Speaks, Volume I: Salt, Light, and Fire from the Sermon That Changed the World
- The Mountain Still Speaks, Volume II: Still He Speaks — Echoes from the Higher Ground, the Narrow Way, the Secret Life, and the Rock That Stands
- God's Sovereignty: Exploring the Divine Rule Over Creation, History, and Eternity
- Divine Encounters: Discovering the Depth and Power of God's Names
- YESHUA: The Nazarene, the Refugee, the Redeemer
- Water Jar: Devotions from the Shadows of Scripture

When he writes, mountains speak again.
And when he signs his name, a generation is being called to higher ground.

www.ingramcontent.com/pod-product-compliance
Lightning Source LLC
Chambersburg PA
CBHW061221070526
44584CB00029B/3928